Nat
Turner

The defiant preacher and self-proclaimed prophet
Nat Turner led the only successful slave uprising in
U.S. history.

JUNIOR ▪ WORLD ▪ BIOGRAPHIES

A JUNIOR *BLACK AMERICANS OF ACHIEVEMENT* BOOK

Nat Turner

ANN-MARIE HENDRICKSON

CHELSEA JUNIORS

a division of CHELSEA HOUSE PUBLISHERS

English-language words that are italicized in the text can be found in the glossary at the back of the book.

Chelsea House Publishers

EDITORIAL DIRECTOR Richard Rennert
EXECUTIVE MANAGING EDITOR Karyn Gullen Browne
COPY CHIEF Robin James
PICTURE EDITOR Adrian G. Allen
CREATIVE DIRECTOR Robert Mitchell
ART DIRECTOR Joan Ferrigno
PRODUCTION MANAGER Sallye Scott

JUNIOR WORLD BIOGRAPHIES

SENIOR EDITOR Martin Schwabacher
SERIES DESIGN Marjorie Zaum

Staff for NAT TURNER

EDITORIAL ASSISTANT Scott D. Briggs
PICTURE RESEARCHER Villette Harris

Copyright © 1995 by Chelsea House Publishers, a division of Main LineBook Co. All rights reserved. Printed and bound in the United States America.

First Printing

1 3 5 7 9 8 6 4 2

Library of Congress Cataloging-in-Publication Data
Hendrickson, Ann-Marie.
  Nat Turner / Ann-Marie Hendrickson
    p. cm.—(Junior world biographies)
  Includes bibliographical references and index.
ISBN 0-7910-2288-9
  0-7910-2289-7 (pbk.)
  1. Turner, Nat, 1800?–1831—Juvenile Literature. 2. Southampton Insurrection, 1831—Juvenile Literature. 3. Slaves—Virginia—Southampton County—Biography—Juvenile literature. I. Title. II. Series.
F232.S7T875 1995
975.5'55203'092—dc20   94-48437
[B]   CIP
                                                                       AC

Contents

Nat Turner's bloody rebellion took the lives of 57 whites and rattled the foundations of the institution of slavery.

1

"I Am Ready"

One Tuesday night in November 1831, a black man, a slave, sat in a room with a white man and told him the story of his life. The white man, a lawyer, carefully wrote down what the black man told him. It was unusual at the time for a white man to listen with such attention to a slave's life story. Generally, a white man would not have found such a tale worthy of his time—and even if he did, the slave probably would not have cared to tell it. But this time, the circumstances were anything but normal. The two men were sitting in a cell in the city jail in Jerusalem, Virginia. It was a few nights before the slave's trial, and the lawyer was taking down the slave's confession. The slave's name was Nat Turner. He was going to trial that Saturday for leading the first successful slave rebellion in American history, a rebellion in which 57 white people had been killed.

One cannot help but wonder what went through Nat Turner's mind as he talked to Thomas Gray, the lawyer. Did he tell the truth about himself, his life, and his friends? Did he wish to explain his actions to the people who were going to judge him and, almost certainly, execute him? Perhaps he felt that this would be his only chance to do so. In that case he was right. For brief as they are, *The Confessions of Nat Turner As Told to Thomas Gray* are almost the only source of information about Nat's life, aside from some crumbling newspaper accounts of the rebellion and the trial. Slaves almost never wrote their own life stories, nor did anyone find it necessary to write down their stories for them. Slave owners were not usually interested in knowing that much about their slaves, and until Nat Turner led a slave rebellion, few whites were interested in knowing that much about him.

That Saturday Nat went to trial. He was convicted of rebellion and murder largely on the strength of his own confession, despite a plea of not guilty. He did not appear to be disturbed or surprised by the verdict.

On Friday, November 11, 1831, Nat Turner was brought in a wagon to the hanging tree, the Southampton County gallows, to be executed. Everyone watching in the large crowd was struck by his cool demeanor and his lack of fear. When the jailer asked him if he had anything to say, he shook his head no. "I am ready," was all he replied. With the same poise he had displayed on his way to the gallows, Nat calmly allowed the rope to be put around his neck. Those watching were shocked to see that he did not twitch or move

On November 11, 1831, at 12:00 P.M., *Nat Turner
was hanged on this tree in Jerusalem, Virginia.*

a muscle, not even when he was jerked off his feet by the rope and hung by the neck until he was dead.

In his brief life, Nat Turner had already told the crowd everything he wanted them to know.

Nat Turner was born a slave on this farm on October 2, 1800. Like the farmhouse itself, Nat was considered the property of Benjamin Turner.

2

A Prophet Born

Nat Turner was born on a farm belonging to Benjamin Turner in Southampton County, Virginia, on October 2, 1800. He was given the last name of Turner because that was the name of his owner. It is likely that the name Nat was not his mother's choice either.

Nat's mother was named Nancy; at least that was what she was called as a slave. She had been captured in Africa just a few years before and had a reputation for being "difficult." She refused to accept her own slavery and was reluctant to learn English. It may be that, like many slaves, she learned English mostly to be able to communicate with other slaves, who came from many different African tribes and did not all speak the same language.

Legend has it that Nancy tried to kill Nat shortly after his birth in order to save him from a life of slavery. The story could well be true; other captured African women are known to have killed their babies for the same reason.

Nancy was considered different from the other slaves around her by white and black people alike. One of the stories told about her in Southampton County was that she had been born a queen among her own people in one of the ancient Egyptian kingdoms of the Nile Valley, where she was captured by Arab slave traders and dragged to the western coast of Africa to be sold to white slave traders. Perhaps people told this story to each other after Nat's rebellion to make the whole account more exciting or to explain how

Nat came to do such extraordinary things. Maybe it was a way of saying that all Africans had had their natural birthright stolen from them when they were seized from their homelands. The word queen may have been used simply because there was no English word to describe her true role. Though many African societies did have powerful rulers, in others the entire community shared responsibility for governing the group.

Of course, it could also be that Nancy was literally a queen, responsible for the well-being of many people. There is no way of knowing, because her background would have been of little interest to the slaveholders who would have kept the only written records of her origins. The fact that so many people believed Nancy to be a queen, however, reveals a great deal about her character and about the way she probably raised her son. One can guess that Nancy encouraged Nat to be fiercely proud of his African blood and that she described to him the beauty of the African landscape, which would have been still fresh in her memory. She probably told of the splendors of the civilization in which she had grown up and the horrors of her violent abduction into slavery. No doubt she related the torment of the Middle Passage, that terrifying journey across the Atlantic in which so many Africans died of disease and starvation. And she must have stressed that as an African, he was born not to be a slave but to live as a free man—exactly the opposite of what his white masters were trying to teach him.

Most of all, one can guess that Nancy taught Nat that he was the descendant of kings and queens and as such had a special mission in life. This could explain why she tried to kill him at birth and why she saved him in the end. If it was humiliating for a prince to live as a slave, at the same time, who better than a prince to free his enslaved people? She probably taught him that a ruler cannot live just for himself and his own good but must take responsibility for the well-being of all his people. She may have raised him to regard himself as an African king in exile, born to teach and protect his people and to lead them out of slavery back into the kingdom in which God intended them to live. One cannot know any of this for certain, but surely the stories about him did not circulate without reason. It was not just his mother's character that gave rise to these legends, but his own.

Nat was recognized as an unusual child from the time he was very young. Great things seem to have been expected of him; he possessed talents no one could explain. Once when Nat was three or four, he began telling the other children a story of something he had seen. His mother, overhearing him, was greatly surprised and told him that he could not possibly have witnessed the event he was describing because it had taken place before he was born. Stubbornly, Nat stuck to his original story. He even added some more details that astounded his mother and the other adults she called in to listen. They were not totally unprepared for his odd behavior, however. Certain marks that Nat had on his head when he was born had served as a sign to the other slaves that God had singled him out for a special purpose. Now they knew what this purpose was. Nat was to be a prophet who possessed precise knowledge of events before his own birth and of events that had yet to come.

Clearly Nat was an unusually intelligent child. All historians agree that he began to read while very young, perhaps before the age of five. Nat himself said that he had learned to read during a vision in which the letters had burned themselves into the fallen leaves upon the ground. Perhaps this is how he experienced it, as though his education were a divine revelation. Perhaps, however, he did not wish to explain how he had learned so that his teacher would not be punished. Some historians believe he may have been educated by his grand-mother, "Old Bridget," a highly intelligent and deeply religious woman who taught Nat about Christianity. Others think he may have been instructed by Benjamin Turner or someone in Turner's family. Benjamin Turner was a liberal Methodist, and the Methodist church officially opposed slavery. Benjamin Turner may have felt guilty about keeping slaves and wished to convert them to Christianity and teach them to read, even if he did not feel he could afford to free them. If so, he was taking a big risk because teaching a slave to read and write was illegal at this time. In any case, Benjamin Turner seems to have been pleased rather than angry that young Nat, a slave, was literate in a time and place in which most free white people were unable to read. He was impressed by Nat's intelligence and remarked that Nat "had too much sense to be raised [as other slaves], and if he was, would never be of any use to anyone as a slave."

When Nat was eight or nine years old, his father ran away from Benjamin Turner's farm. No one really knows what happened to him after that. Some said he escaped to the North or back to

Africa. Others speculated that he was captured and killed. Young Nat never knew what happened to his father, and one can only guess at his feelings.

Like most slaves, Nat was put to work in the fields at age 12. Conditions on the farm in southern Virginia were not as harsh as they were

A map of southeastern Virginia shows Southampton County. Turner grew up just southwest of the town of Jerusalem.

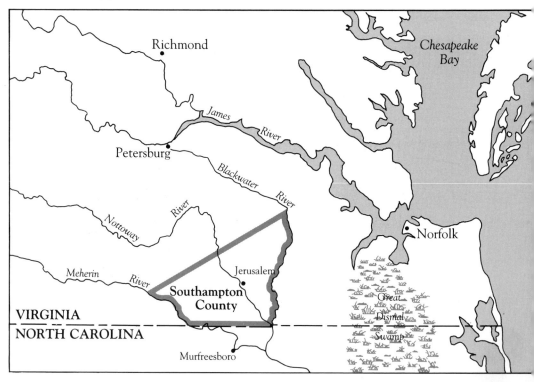

in the Deep South. In the giant plantations of Louisiana, Alabama, Georgia, and Mississippi, slaves had a far more difficult life than in Virginia. Like most other small farmers in Virginia, the Turners often worked in the fields alongside their slaves. Still, the work was exhausting, and Nat knew that no matter how hard he labored, he was not working for himself or for anyone in his family. Everything he did would be for his owners' benefit.

On his own time, Nat read fervently the one book that his master approved of: the Bible. Most slave owners believed Christianity would make their slaves more willing to accept their fate. But Nat's profound religious feelings had the opposite effect. He did not become a more docile slave. Instead he came to believe even more strongly that God had chosen him, Nat, to be a prophet who would lead his people out of slavery, just as God had chosen the prophets of the Old Testament to lead the Jews out of slavery in ancient times. Nat took this calling very seriously, and it seems that all the blacks in the surrounding area, both free and enslaved, took it very seriously as well. Nat became famous locally for his intelligence, his wisdom, and his honesty. Even as a child, other children consulted him. Although he was not interested in thievery or mischief, he was frequently asked to help plan the schemes of others.

In his *Confessions,* Nat said that one day when he was a teenager, while working behind a plow, he heard a voice saying, "Seek ye the kingdom of Heaven and all things shall be added unto you." There was no doubt in his mind that he was hearing the voice of God, the God that had spoken to the kings and prophets of the Old Testament. This strengthened his feeling of being singled out for important things.

When Nat was about 20 years old, an economic depression hit Virginia, making it more difficult for slave owners to make a profit. Samuel Turner, who had inherited Nat from his father, Benjamin, hired a new overseer to work the slaves even harder. The new overseer was so harsh that Nat ran away. After 30 days, to the astonishment of everyone, Nat returned to the farm. His owner was so amazed by Nat's return that he decided not to punish him. The other slaves felt that Nat should have followed the example of his father and never returned. But his own freedom was clearly not enough for him, not when so many others were still in bondage. Nat did not explain his reasoning to anyone at the time. In his *Confessions,* he said that God had instructed him to return: "the Spirit appeared to me and said I had my wishes directed to the things of this world, and not to the kingdom of Heaven, and that I should return to the service of my earthly master—'For he who knoweth his Master's will, and doeth it not, shall be beaten with many stripes, and thus have I chastened you.'" In any case, Nat's reputation for integrity was increased by this incident. Only a man who felt some responsibility for easing the situation of his people would have even considered returning to a condition of slavery after escaping.

Sometime in 1822, Nat married a slave named Cherry. Later that same year, Samuel Turner died. Nat's mother remained on the Turner farm, while Nat was sold to a neighbor, Samuel Moore. Cherry was sold to a different neighbor, Giles Reese. Once again, one can only imagine Nat's feelings about this catastrophe, over which he had no control. Newly married, he was unable to see his wife when he wished or to protect her from harm.

In 1825, Nat's visions became more frequent. According to his *Confessions,* he saw "white spirits and black spirits engaged in battle, and the sun was darkened—the thunder rolled in the heavens, and blood flowed in streams—and I heard a voice saying, 'Such is your luck, such you are called to see, and let it come rough or smooth, you must surely bear it.'" He heard the Holy Spirit tell him that it would reveal "the knowledge of the elements, the revolution of the planets, the operation of tides, and changes of the seasons." Nat felt that he had to prepare himself all the more for his task. He began to withdraw more and more from the usual friendly amusements of his fellow slaves, devoting himself to prayer and meditation.

During this period Nat served as a preacher in a black Methodist church. His reputation was such that slaves and free blacks from throughout the county would gather to hear him preach on the Sundays that his owners allowed him to go. The contacts he made while doing this must have enabled him to organize his rebellion. No doubt some who involved themselves were only pretending to be religious in order to meet and talk with their fellow slaves. But many were inspired by their religion to believe that slavery was evil and that God favored their struggle for freedom. The quick response of slaves and free blacks to Nat's call during the uprising suggests that the level of organization that developed among interested black people was very high indeed. Much of this organization took place within the meetings of the black churches and, in many cases, under the noses of the white slave owners.

In any event, Nat was highly regarded in Southampton County by everyone who knew him, both black and white. He would not drink, smoke, or curse. He did not involve himself in gambling or in "conjure" (magic or sorcery) tricks, for which he had great contempt. He wished to inspire people on the basis of his preaching and not on the basis of magic.

After his vision of black spirits battling white spirits, Nat continued to see signs that the judgment day was at hand. He later wrote in his *Confessions:*

> I wondered greatly at these miracles, and prayed to be informed of a certainty of the meaning thereof—and shortly afterwards, while laboring in the field, I discovered drops of blood on the corn as though it were dew from heaven—and I communicated it to many, both white and black, in the neighborhood—and I then found on the leaves in the woods hieroglyphic characters, and numbers, with the forms of men in different attitudes, portrayed in blood, and representing the figures I had seen before in the heavens.

Nat warned his neighbors that the blood of Christ was returning to earth. He said, "it was plain to me that the Saviour was about to lay down the yoke he had borne for the sins of men, and the great day of judgment was at hand."

One white man who heard him preach, Etheldred T. Brantley, was so impressed that he begged Nat to baptize him as a Methodist. The white people refused to allow a black man to baptize a white man in their church, so the baptism took place in a local river. There, before a crowd of angry, taunting onlookers, the two were "baptised by the Spirit." Despite the hostile crowd, Nat "rejoiced greatly, and gave thanks to God."

Nat Turner laid the groundwork for his rebellion by preaching at local churches including this one, the Southampton Methodist Church.

CHAPTER

3

A Sign
from God

On May 12, 1828, Nat had a new vision. He
recalled in his *Confessions*:

> I heard a loud noise in the heavens, and the Spirit
> instantly appeared to me and said the Serpent was
> loosened, and Christ had laid down the yoke he had
> borne for the sins of men, and that I should take it
> on and fight against the Serpent, for the time was
> fast approaching when the first should be last and
> the last should be first.

To Nat, this clearly meant that the time was coming when the slaves would rise up against their masters. He was instructed to wait for a further, clearer sign that the moment for his great work had arrived.

In the meantime, Nat continued preaching to black people about his visions of judgment and freedom. On his free days he traveled throughout the county from one prayer meeting to the next. He was always welcomed as a much respected prophet and holy man, a possessor of unusual and divinely given knowledge. In this way Nat continued to prepare for the great moment he was certain would soon arrive. He knew he would need a trustworthy and organized group of men and women to carry out the plan that God would reveal to him. Nat's experiences in the churches showed him who shared his faith and who did not, who was courageous and reliable and who was not. Nat bided his time and continued to work in the fields. He knew that God would clearly reveal to him his destiny, as He had been doing all along, if only Nat would continue to prepare himself and remember his mission and his responsibilities.

Later that same year, Samuel Moore died, and Nat was given to yet another master. Nat and Moore's 16 other slaves passed to his nine-year-old son, Putnam Moore, and then to Joseph Travis when he married Samuel Moore's widow, Sally, in October 1829.

But none of the events in Nat's personal life had as large an effect on him as the great solar eclipse of February 1831. This eclipse was widely seen throughout the country as a warning of calamitous, perhaps apocalyptic events. To Nat, it served as the heavenly sign he had awaited to begin preparing for his work of making, as the Bible said, the first the last and the last the first. The slaves referred to this as the Jubilee. In the Old Testament of the Bible, the festival of Jubilee was said to come every 50 years, at which point all land would be returned to common ownership, all debts would be forgiven, and all slaves would be freed. In the highly religious society of Southampton County in the 1830s, this idea of the Jubilee would have been well known to everyone, both white and black. To Nat Turner, prepared as he had been for his entire life to help bring about the Jubilee and the liberation of the slaves, the eclipse was a direct order. It was an order he had been expecting for years.

It is believed that at this time Nat Turner began to gather his confederates and plan his rebellion. Years of living, working, and preaching

In his rousing sermons, Nat Turner preached that the day of judgment was at hand and that the enslaved blacks would soon be free.

in the county had given him the chance to decide who he could trust to go along with him and who would betray him. The sign from God himself in the heavens showed that the time for action was close at hand. Now, Nat only had to plan his strategy.

It appears that Nat chose about 20 men to rise up with him. Such was the sophistication of his organization that to this day the names of only

seven or eight of them are known. In his *Confessions,* Nat named only those who had already been captured. It seems likely that Nat's wife, Cherry, was involved in the planning. After the rebellion, she was tortured under the lash in order to make her surrender Nat's papers. His secret papers were of little use to his enemies, however, because they were written in code in pokeberry juice and were never deciphered.

Of his chief co-conspirators, four are known. First, there was Hark Travis, Hark being short for Hercules. He was described as very proud and strong, a "regular black Apollo." Next was Nelson Williams, rumored to be a conjure man and a healer with the gift of prophecy. Little is known of the other two, Sam Francis and Henry Porter, other than that they lived on neighboring farms. Probably there were many more whom Nat did not care to reveal in his confession.

The original plan was to act on July 4, 1831—ironically, the United States's own Independence Day. But Nat was sick and no final plan had been selected, so they decided to wait. On Saturday, August 13, a darkness passed over the sky, making it possible to look at the sun directly. The sun seemed to change from green to blue to white. This marvel could be seen along the entire eastern seaboard and alarmed a great many people, both black and white. Shortly afterward a black spot appeared on the sun. "Just as the black spot passed over the sun, so shall the blacks pass over the earth," said Nat to his co-conspirators. Plans were made, and the word was spread. Later testimony in the trial records indicate that there was a great deal of talk and activity among the slaves of the county in the following week. On Thursday, August 18, Nelson Williams was reported to have walked up to his overseer and announced that the white people should "look out and take care of themselves, that something would happen before long."

On Sunday, August 21, 1831, Hark, Nelson, Henry, and Sam were having a pig roast in a field near Cabin Pond, drinking the apple brandy for which Southampton County was famous and enjoying the smell of the barbecue. Along with them were two new recruits, Jack Reese and Will Francis. Nat let them wait for him a while, adding to the air of distance and mystery he had cultivated since childhood. He joined them at about three o'clock in the afternoon, and together they made the final plans for the rebellion. It was decided that they would begin that very night. Their plan was to rise up and "kill all the white people" while moving toward the Southampton County seat, fittingly named Jerusalem. It was in the biblical city of Jerusalem, according to the Old Testament prophet Ezekiel, that God had ordered every man, woman, and child who did not obey him to be killed without mercy. Nat was certain that similar orders were now being given to him.

Nat Turner was ready to begin the work for which he had prepared his entire life. He felt that God himself was ordering the beginning of this war, that God intended him to take up arms against the enemies of his people. He must have remembered God's words in the book of Ezekiel: "Go through the midst of the city, through the midst of Jerusalem, and set a mark upon the foreheads of the men that sigh and that cry for all the abominations that be done in the midst thereof." To Nat, this meant he should spare the slaves and poor whites and those sympathetic to the cause of the slaves. As for the others, the slaveholders who bought and sold and worked human beings as though they were animals, the Bible's words were clear: "'Go ye after him through the city, and smite,' said Jehovah, 'Let not your eye spare, neither have ye pity: slay utterly old and young, both maids and little children, and women: but come not near any man upon whom is the mark; and begin at my sanctuary. Defile the house, and fill the courts with the slain: go ye forth.' And they went forth, and slew in the city."

In the dark of night, at around 2:00 A.M. on August 22, 1832, Nat Turner gathered his men to begin their bloody work.

4

In Bloody
Battle

The rebellion began on August 22, 1831, at 2 A.M. Nat and the others met in the courtyard of the Travis farm and were joined by two newcomers, Austin and Moses. All but Nat calmed themselves with a drink of cider. (Later, Nat would have cause to regret that he allowed his army to drink alcohol during a military operation.) Hark suggested breaking into the house with an axe, but Nat wanted to remain quiet and keep the element of surprise for as long as possible. A ladder was placed against the side of the house, and Nat climbed through the window into the upstairs bedroom of his own masters. He crept downstairs to unlock the door, and his friends joined him inside.

The raiders agreed that Prophet Nat should deliver the first blow in their war. Nat raised a hatchet and struck a blow against the head of Joseph Travis, who leaped out of bed and began to yell. Will took his own weapon and finished off both the master and the mistress. The rebellion had begun.

One by one, all the white inhabitants of the house were killed in their beds. In his *Confessions,* Nat said that his instructions were to spare neither age nor sex (in keeping with the Biblical instructions in the book of Ezekiel). In accordance with this principle, a baby who had been temporarily forgotten was killed by Henry and Will before they left the farm. The rebel slaves took some guns and ammunition from the farm before they left. Nat stressed to them, as he did throughout the rebellion, that they were not merely pirates or marauders but a liberating force. He was a king and a prophet risen up to free his people, as in the days of Moses and Aaron, and they were his army. Nat Turner had not engaged in looting and thievery even as a child, and he was not going to engage in it now that he had grown to act upon his adult responsibilites. He would not allow his men to forget that they were soldiers, not common thieves and criminals. They were not to take anything from the farmhouses that they did not need for their military operation, nor were they to torture or rape their victims. By all accounts, even those of their enemies, these rules were strictly followed. The insurrection was bloody but not wanton or sadistic.

The next stop was the farm of Sally Travis's brother, Salathial, and the same plan was followed: all the white inhabitants were killed, guns and ammunition were taken, and some of the black slaves were recruited to join the rebellion. Though the insurgents were gathering firearms at each stop, they did not use guns at first because they did not want to wake up the neighbors. Throughout the night, the rebels traveled from farm to farm on their way to Jerusalem, the county seat, and at each farm their force grew without any of the white population being alarmed. At each house, the white people were killed without exception, and all willing slaves were taken on as recruits. The others were warned not to interfere.

By daybreak Nat had gathered together a company of 15 armed men, including 9 on horseback. This force was large enough that Nat ordered them to split up into smaller groups and continue with "the work of death" until they would rejoin by midmorning. The people of the county were beginning to wake up, but opposition still had not been organized. This situation would not last long, as Nat well knew, and it was important that his army gain as much territory as possible before the counterattack began. By the time Nat's forces had arrived at the Porter farm, just a few miles down the road, they found the homestead deserted. Nat realized that the surprise attack was over, as the inhabitants had clearly been warned about the uprising. The battle was now going to escalate into a full-pitched war.

By 10 o'clock in the morning a force of about 40 armed men under General Nat's command had gathered at the Harris farm, some five miles from Jerusalem. By noon there would be more than 60 of them. But trouble was already in store for the rebels. Discipline was breaking down, partly from the excitement of the victories already achieved and partly from the drunkenness of some of the fighters who had been celebrating with brandy and cider along the way, in opposition to Nat's strict orders. More important, the county had begun to stir and the telegraph lines were beginning to hum. Messengers on horseback were racing toward the state capitol at Richmond. It would not be long until all the whites in the area would be up in arms to crush the slave rebellion.

What was Nat Turner's plan? Now that he had gathered his army and had begun to move across Southampton County toward Jerusalem, where did he hope to go from there? Many white people at the time thought he might have planned to lead his men into the Great Dismal Swamp, some 20 miles to the east. The swamp was a desolate wilderness where many runaway slaves chose to hide. Many had in fact been able to live there for years without being caught. But what then? There would hardly seem to have been any point to such a bloody and savage war unless he were planning to return and occupy the area. The farms themselves were not damaged in any way, although they easily could have been burned. There must have been some hope among the rebel slaves to return and reclaim the farms that they themselves had built and worked. If the farms belonged to anyone, was it not to them?

The white militia in Jerusalem was already in action by noon on Monday, August 22. Rumors were flying around the county. Remembering the War of 1812 against England, some slave owners panicked, believing that the British had invaded

Southampton County and had again declared war on the United States. The truth, when they discovered it, was even more frightening: General Nat had declared war on the white people, and the black population was rising up en masse to join him. Justice James Trezevant of the Southampton County Court sent out an urgent message by express rider: "Terrible insurrection; several families obliterated. Send arms and men at once; a large force may be needed." Word was rapidly sent out not just to the state capitol at Richmond but to the federal government in Washington as well. A slave rebellion was the secret nightmare of every white southerner. This was why they were so quick to organize. They had lived in constant fear of a slave revolt, despite their arguments in favor of the slave system. Thirty years earlier, a slave named Gabriel Prosser had barely been prevented from carrying out a similar slave rebellion in Virginia. He had been betrayed by other slaves, and this had reassured the slave owners that most slaves would never participate in such an uprising but would report it to the proper authorities. Now it was clear that they had been sitting on a powder keg the entire time. The people they had used and abused, the people they had beaten and mis-treated, the people they had stolen from their own homeland and worked like animals—these people had now turned the tables on their owners. Virginia was at war.

By noon, Nat and his men could see the city of Jerusalem. They watched the smoke rising from the fires and heard the urgent ringing of the church bells. The entire county was awake and alarmed. Nat knew that soon his army would have to engage in open battle with the white militia. He must have hoped that there was still a chance that he and his men could seize the town of Jerusalem. There, with food, fresh ammunition, and better arms, they could hold out until more slaves and free blacks joined them.

At the Parker farm on Barrow Road, just a few miles from the county seat, Nat and the rebels met a detachment of white militia, about 18 in number. Seeing that his men were alarmed by their first encounter with enemy troops, Nat ordered them to halt and assume battle formation. The militiamen approached to within about 100 yards, and when a white soldier fired the first shot, Nat ordered his men to charge. The white soldiers

The rebels marched from house to house toward Jerusalem until they were forced back by the militia.

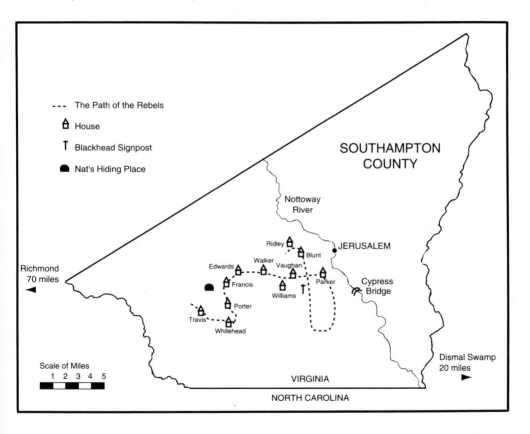

retreated, and their attackers chased them about 200 yards up a small hill, overtaking and wounding several of them.

Unfortunately for the rebels, another group of armed men was in the area searching for the slave army. When they heard gunfire, they rushed to join the battle. Several of Nat's best fighters were wounded, and the others began to panic as the whites chased and shot at them. When Hark's horse was shot out from under him, Nat grabbed another horse for him as it ran by. All in all, five or six members of the outnumbered black forces were injured, but they managed to escape without leaving anybody behind.

The slaves retreated a couple of miles into the forest along the Nottoway River. From there, Nat attempted to lead his forces along a back road to attack Jerusalem from another direction. By the time they reached Cypress Bridge, they saw that their luck had begun to run out. The bridge was full of armed white militia. Nat decided to retreat still further to the Ridley farm to rest, regroup, and gather more recruits. From farm to farm the rebels fought, retreated, and hid, but numbers and exhaustion were working against them.

That night, one of Nat's sentinels mistakenly reported that they were about to be overrun by white militiamen. As the rebels milled around in the dark, no one could tell who was who, and several ran away, thinking they were under attack. By morning, Nat's forces had been reduced from about 40 to barely 20.

By Monday night, white militia were pouring into Southampton County. By Tuesday morning, the militia were coming not just from neighboring counties in Virginia but from nearby North Carolina as well. Knowing there was a company of men at Major Ridley's, Nat's men approached the farm of Dr. Blunt. Hark fired his gun to see if anyone in Dr. Blunt's family was at home. To their complete surprise, a barrage of bullets came from the house. At the orders of their master, some of Blunt's slaves inside the building joined in the gunfire. Caught off guard, several of

Nat hoped to attack the town of Jerusalem by crossing the Nottoway River at Cypress Bridge, shown here. When he reached the bridge, however, he found it guarded by armed militiamen.

Nat's men fell wounded, including Hark. The survivors had no choice but to leave their comrades behind and flee for their lives.

By 10:00 A.M. Tuesday morning, the rebels had retreated back to the Harris farm, only a few miles from where they had started. This was to be the site of their final rout. Nat's exhausted men were no match for the fresh militiamen, with their superior weapons and ammunition. As one rebel after another was killed, Nat ordered a retreat and went into hiding.

Along with his last four men, Nat made his way back to the Travis farm where the whole insurrection had begun. He sent the two least exhausted rebels to spread the word to regroup the next day. Tuesday night he rested and waited. Then, on Wednesday morning, he sent out his last two men to gather more soldiers. But time had run out for Nat. By Tuesday afternoon the army had moved into Southampton County and the navy was on its way.

By the time Nat went into hiding at the Travis farm, half of his men had been killed and most of the survivors had gone into hiding. Slowly but surely, the rebels began to be captured, 59 in all during the next 10 days. But no one could find Nat Turner.

A woodcut shows Nat at the moment of his capture, still carrying the sword he used during his revolt.

CHAPTER

5

Wanted:
Nat Turner

By the end of August, Nat must have been aware that, at least for the moment, his rebellion had failed. What did he hope for at that moment, while in hiding? He must have felt discouragement, maybe even despair. Was this the fate for which God had been preparing him? Was this the destiny for which his proud mother had raised him? Was he planning to gather more men and go hide in the Great Dismal Swamp, as some thought later? Did he hope to rejoin his family and take them with him? Did he hope that the setback was only temporary, something he might wait out and survive? Surely he must have been planning a way to continue the insurrection. Perhaps he hoped that more slaves would rise up against their masters and come to his aid.

Whatever his thoughts at the time, there is no question that Nat's hiding was extraordinarily effective. After coming to the conclusion that all of his followers had been captured, he gave up his hopes for the present but made no attempt to leave the area. Instead, he recalled in his confession:

> After having supplied myself with provisions from Mr. Travis's, I scratched a hole under a pile of fence rails in a field, where I concealed myself for six weeks, never leaving my hiding place but for a few minutes in the dead of night to get water which was very near; thinking by this time I could venture out, I began to go about in the night and eavesdrop the houses in the neighborhood.

By early September, wanted posters advertising a reward of over a thousand dollars for the capture of the "great banditti chief" Nat Turner papered the county—and still he was not caught. On the posters, Nat was described as "between 30 and 35 years old—five feet six or eight inches high—weighs between 150 and 160—rather bright complexion but not a mulatto—broad-shouldered—large flat nose—large eyes—broad flat feet rather knock kneed—walk brisk and active—hair on the top of the head very thin—no beard except on the upper lip and the top of the chin." Surely he must have had some help from sympathetic slaves and free blacks as he hid out in the woods. The fact that Nat was able to elude capture for so long would seem to indicate that this was the case. The great underground slave organization may have failed to overthrow the government, but it had not entirely ceased to function.

Perhaps Nat was waiting for a sign from heaven as to how to proceed. He did not abandon his sword, so he must not have given up his hopes for success. One might guess that he contacted his wife, although not openly to keep from endangering her. Certainly his life had become very dangerous by then. Once, two slaves caught sight of him while they were out hunting and betrayed him to their masters; Nat barely escaped the posse that came after him. Soon afterward, a man shot at him and put a hole through his hat. A second posse began to hunt him. Still, Nat managed to avoid being captured for a full two months.

On October 30, a man named Benjamin Phipps, out hunting with his dog, came upon Nat in his cave and ordered him to surrender. In his *Confessions*, Nat says that he decided it would be better to surrender than to face the kind of vigilante justice that would inevitably follow were he to continue to fight.

Why did he not attempt to leave the county? Probably for the same reason that he returned to his owner after running away so many years before. He did not value his own personal survival as much as he valued the liberation of all his people. Also, he must certainly have felt it would be cowardly of him to survive through stealth and cunning a war in which so many of his fellow rebels had been killed. For better or for worse, he felt it his responsibility to stay. As the Holy Spirit had revealed to him all those years before, "Such is your luck, such you are called to see, and let it come rough or smooth, you must surely bear it." Nat's path was becoming very rough indeed, but he would be brave and bear it.

After his capture, Nat Turner was brought in chains to Jerusalem, where he was met by a crowd of people who mocked him, threatened him, and spit in his face. He was questioned, arraigned, and brought to trial. He made his confession, expressing no remorse for the deaths of the 57 white people killed in the rebellion. To the end, he maintained that he had acted under the orders of God. He insisted that he regretted only the failure of his rebellion, and that if he had it all to do over again, he "must necessarily act in the same way."

On November 1, the lawyer Thomas Gray was permitted to enter Nat's cell. He wished to obtain from Nat a true account of what had taken place. Gray may also have wanted to cash in on the notoriety of the case and the public hysteria surrounding the rebellion. Within a few days, *The Confessions of Nat Turner As Told to Thomas Gray* was available for sale as a pamphlet. One historian estimated that a total of 50,000 copies were eventually sold, which must have earned Gray a pretty penny.

Nat Turner's trial took place in this courthouse. He was convicted and sentenced to death by hanging.

What Nat's motivations were in talking to Gray cannot be known. The confession seems straightforward enough, but why would Nat have wished to make one? Perhaps by that point he was most concerned about having his motivations understood. Both in the *Confessions* and in his court testimony he stressed the seriousness of his purpose and the divine origins of his inspirations. He was not concerned with attempting to prove his innocence in any way. He could not have had any hopes of escaping execution, but he had no regrets.

When Nat told Gray of his prophetic visions that the Judgment Day was near, Gray interrupted him to ask, "Do you not find yourself mistaken now?" After all, Nat was in jail awaiting execution, and his rebellion had been decisively crushed. Nat, defiant to the end, answered, "Was not Christ crucified?"

Nat appears to have decided to face death as bravely as Jesus had, like a martyr. He would be executed, and seemingly, that would be the end of his story. But was it?

After the rebellion was crushed, furious whites flocked into Southampton County, randomly killing any blacks they could find. This crossroads is known as Blackhead Signpost because the head of a black man was displayed here on a pole.

CHAPTER

6

The Call
of Freedom

The impact of Nat Turner's rebellion continued to rattle the foundations of the institution of slavery long after his death. For slave owners, the fear that had always been in the back of their minds was abruptly made into a reality. For years they had argued that slaves were unsuited for freedom, and that they were, for the most part, happy and satisfied with their own enslavement. They had tried to convince themselves that Africans were simply too cowardly and passive to carry out a revolt and too childlike to be able to plan one. It was clear now that none of this was true. The success of Nat Turner, plus the frighteningly large number of slaves and free blacks involved in the revolt, made clear the extent of slave discontent and the ability of slaves to fight back.

Everywhere the slave owners looked, they saw how dependent they were on blacks to work the land, produce goods, and suffer without complaint. Could they continue to rely on these people? Could it happen that the slave who slept in her master's house, who cooked and cleaned and took care of his children, might arise one night without warning and kill her owners? Suddenly, white slave owners throughout Virginia were terrified.

The first reaction of many white people in Southampton County was to teach all blacks a lesson. Black people throughout the area were brutally attacked by vigilantes determined to avenge the deaths of Nat Turner's victims. Black families were pulled out of their homes by angry mobs. Blacks were tortured, whipped, and killed. Businesses owned by free blacks were burned and looted. One man boasted to a local paper that he had shot fifteen blacks in two days and hoped to shoot more. One army unit killed 40 black people and impaled their heads on poles along the road. As many as 200 blacks were murdered. The situation became so bad that General Eppes, the army commander called in to pacify the area, declared that any further atrocities would be treated as war crimes.

The state of Virginia wanted to deal with the rebellion in a legal and orderly way and not permit local whites to take the law into their own hands. But blacks did not face a much friendlier atmosphere inside the courts of law than they did outside with the lynch mobs. The 49 blacks who were imprisoned on suspicion of having participated in the rebellion were being judged by white judges and white juries who were sympathetic to the white victims and probably knew some of them personally. Most of the witnesses who testified against the accused rebels were slaves themselves (slaves could appear as witnesses but not serve as jurors). Many of these slave witnesses, like Nat Turner's own wife, were whipped and tortured into giving evidence. Probably many, perhaps most, were forced to testify or were afraid they would be punished along with the rebels if they did not. The court-appointed lawyers took little interest in trying to defend their clients. More time was spent at the trials establishing the dollar value of each slave than in determining their guilt or innocence. Before any slave could be executed, his or her price had to be settled by the court so that the state could compensate the owner for the loss.

The trials went on for weeks. All in all, about 20 men (and a few women) were convicted and hanged. Most of the others accused were deported to even more brutal plantations in the Caribbean and Deep South.

But the uproar did not die down after the trials and executions were over. The slave owners were so afraid of another successful revolt that in

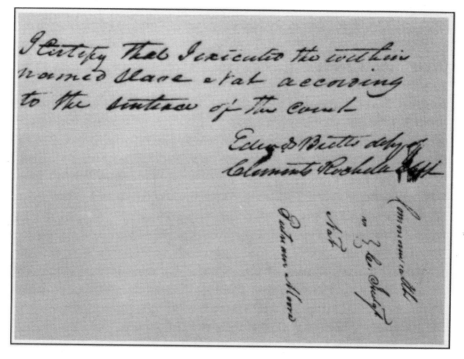

After his execution, Nat Turner became a symbol of the slaves' determination to win their freedom. His death certificate is shown here.

late 1831 the Virginia legislature debated whether or not to continue to allow slavery in Virginia. Many white people came forward to suggest that slavery should be abolished. Some favored abolition because they felt that slavery was cruel and morally wrong, but most expressed the fear that it was dangerous to keep slaves who might revolt at any moment and kill their masters. Others were concerned about the large numbers of free black people in Virginia. They were afraid that the free blacks, most of whom had parents, husbands, wives, or other family members who were enslaved, would join in future slave revolts, just as many had done with Nat Turner. It was suggested that all free blacks be deported from the state. Another plan was to make both slaves and free blacks work for the state until they had earned enough money to pay for their forced deportation from Virginia. This way, no slave owners would be required to lose money.

At the end of these debates, slavery was retained and blacks were not deported. Instead, extremely severe laws were passed restricting the freedom of black people to speak, worship, and assemble. The slave system continued, but the slave owners could no longer pretend that the system was working smoothly. They were made even more aware that if they wanted to own other human beings and keep them as slaves, they could do so only by force. And they were afraid that they might not possess the necessary strength to continue to do so.

In Virginia and throughout the country, many slaves were having similar thoughts. In Dorchester County, Maryland, only 100 miles away from the revolt, 11-year-old Harriet Tubman was working as a slave and already dreaming of freedom. In Baltimore, 13-year-old Frederick Douglass was doing the same thing. Both grew up to be famous crusaders against slavery and both later wrote about the inspiration they had derived from Nat Turner's revolt. In the fields at work, in their shacks, and in their clandestine churches, slaves managed to talk to each other about the revolt. Just as the slave owners had been unable to keep the slaves from planning the revolt, they were unable to keep the slaves from telling each other about it. In fact, Nat Turner began to become an even more powerful figure in death than he had been in life. His very name became symbolic of slave retribution, and as such he became a legendary hero for southern black people. "Prophet Nat," who fooled the white master while he planned his revolution, joined the other heroes of black folklore.

In the North, the abolitionist movement was greatly expanded in the wake of the publicity of the revolt. William Lloyd Garrison, editor of the famous abolitionist newspaper the *Liberator,* was saddened by the violence on both sides, but he felt that the cruelty of slavery itself made such bloody revolts inevitable. He hoped that Nat Turner's actions would make more Americans realize that slavery should be abolished. Many did, and thousands joined the northern anti-slavery societies at this time. The circulation of anti-slavery newspapers such as the *Liberator* increased so dramatically that southern states passed laws making it illegal for anyone to subscribe to them or to distribute copies to anyone, black or white. In 1834, slavery was legally abolished in England, further limiting the world slave trade.

Nat Turner's revolt sent out shock waves that were felt for years to come. Three decades later, the United States fought a long and bloody Civil War, largely over the issue of slavery. In black folklore, the Civil War, which ended slavery in the United States, was called the "Second War." The "First War" against slavery was Nat Turner's revolt.

Further Reading

Banta, Melissa. *Frederick Douglass: Voice of Liberty.* New York: Chelsea House, 1993.

Bisson, Terry. *Nat Turner: Slave Revolt Leader.* New York: Chelsea House, 1988.

Burns, Bree. *Harriet Tubman and the Fight Against Slavery.* New York: Chelsea House, 1992.

Feinberg, Brian. *Nelson Mandela and the Quest for Freedom.* New York: Chelsea House, 1992.

Hoobler, Thomas, and Dorothy Hoobler. *Toussaint L'Ouverture.* New York: Chelsea House, 1990.

Macht, Norman L. *Sojourner Truth: Crusader for Civil Rights.* New York: Chelsea House, 1992.

Shirley, David. *Malcolm X: Minister of Justice.* New York: Chelsea House, 1994.

Glossary

---

abduction kidnapping or carrying a person off by force

arraign call before a court and formally charge with a crime

baptize to spiritually purify or cleanse someone with water as part of the Christian ritual of baptism

catastrophe a major disaster

clandestine meeting in secret

confederates partners

confession a formal statement admitting one's crimes and explaining one's actions or beliefs

contempt scorn or disgust; lack of respect

cultivate to develop or assist the growth of

decipher   decode

eclipse   a shadow passing over the sun or moon, as when the moon passes in front of the sun, temporarily blocking it from view

en masse   as a whole; together as one

execute   to put to death as a legal punishment

hieroglyphic   part of a system of writing based on pictures

inevitable   unavoidable; to be expected

integrity   following a strict moral code

meditation   thinking deeply; reflecting on spiritual matters

militia   an army that is summoned only during emergencies

plantation   a large farm that depends on a group of laborers who live and work there

profound   deeply felt or thought

prophet   a person who can predict the future or receive messages from God

retribution   striking back; punishment

speculate   to wonder or suppose

vision   a mystical experience in which one sees a supernatural image revealing a religious or spiritual truth

Chronology

October 2, 1800	Nat Turner is born a slave in Southampton County, Virginia, the property of Benjamin Turner
c. 1821	Runs away from farm of Samuel Turner (Benjamin Turner's son); returns voluntarily after 30 days; marries a slave named Cherry
c. 1822	Samuel Turner dies; Nat is sold to Thomas Moore, separating him from his wife
c. 1825	Nat has first mystical vision; becomes a preacher; baptizes a white man in a river
May 12, 1828	Nat has second vision

1830	After Thomas Moore's death, his widow marries Joseph Travis, and Nat is moved to Travis's home
August 13, 1831	Sun appears unusual; Nat considers this a sign from God to begin revolt
August 21, 1831	Nat assembles a group of slaves to plan raid
August 22, 1831	Nat leads rebels from house to house, killing every white person they encounter; the numbers swell as more slaves join the uprising
August 23, 1831	After a final battle, most of Nat's men are killed or captured; Nat goes into hiding
October 30, 1831	Nat is discovered in a cave and captured
November 1– 3, 1831	Thomas Gray interviews Nat and writes down his confessions
November 5, 1831	Nat is tried and sentenced to death

November 11, 1831	Nat is executed by hanging
November 1831	Gray publishes Nat's confessions as a pamphlet; about 50,000 copies are eventually sold

Index

Ann-Marie Hendrickson grew up in Los Angeles, California and graduated from the University of California at Santa Cruz before moving to New York City, where she works for the New York Public Library. She has edited several independent publications, and her writing has appeared in magazines including *Rock Against Sexism* and *Processed World*. She also volunteers for political organizations such as Neither East Nor West, of which she is a founding member.

PICTURE CREDITS

B
TUR
   Hendrickson, Ann-Marie
   Nat Turner

DATE DUE			
5/24/96		DEC 06 1999	